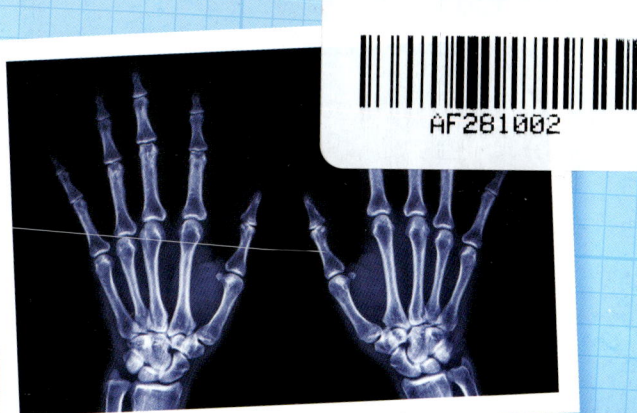

Skelebones

Dr Ranj Singh

Illustrated by **David Semple**

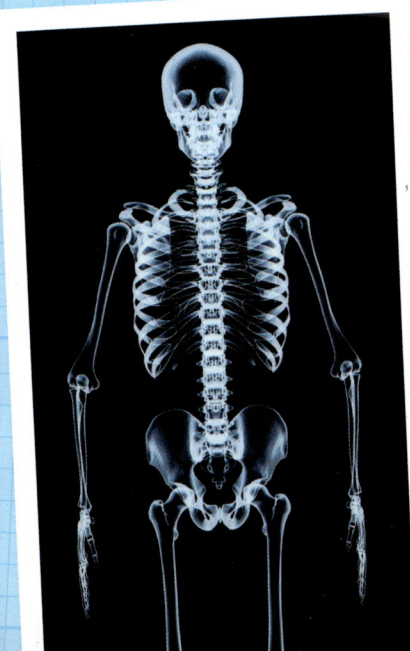

OXFORD
UNIVERSITY PRESS

Contents

What is a Skeleton?

A skeleton is an amazing collection of bones inside the body. We each have one. They come in all different shapes and sizes. Lots of animals have skeletons too.

What would happen if you didn't have a skeleton?

Some animals, such as jellyfish, don't have a skeleton. Without your skeleton you would also be a floppy pile of jelly on the floor!

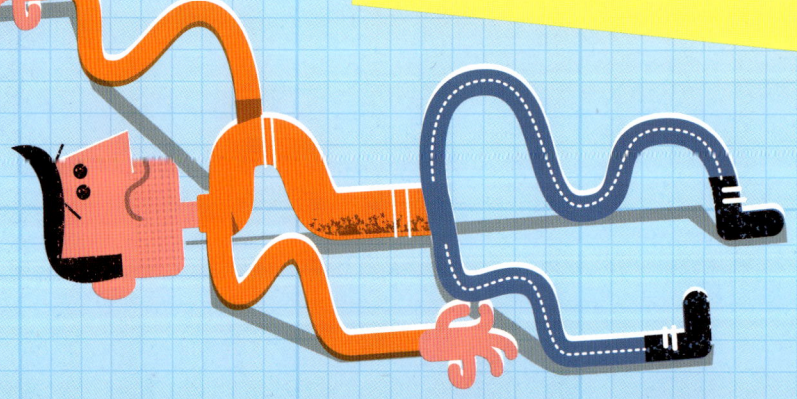

Your clever skeleton ...

1 holds you up – like scaffolding around a building

2 lets you move around, using your joints and **muscles**

3 heals itself when it breaks

4 protects the different **organs** inside your body, like a suit of armour

5 grows and changes shape as you get older.

Let's look inside the body using our special skeleton scanner!

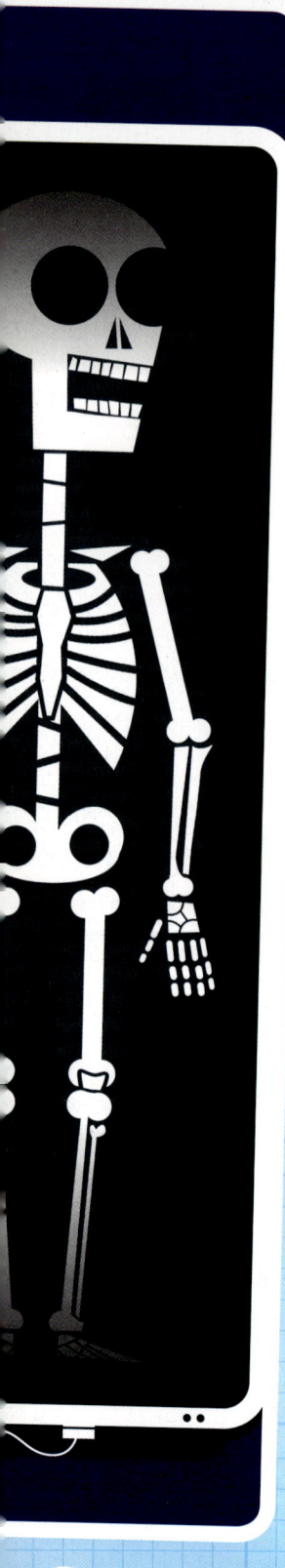

How to Build a Bone

Each of your bones has its own name, from the big bones in your legs to the tiny ones in your ears!

Most of your bones are made in exactly the same way. They start off as slightly squashy stuff called **cartilage**.

This cartilage then becomes harder and turns into proper bone. Your body uses something called **calcium** to make cartilage hard.

Skelefact!

Shark skeletons are all cartilage. That makes them light and flexible!

Babies are born with over 300 different bones. Lots of them are made of cartilage.

As you grow, your bones get bigger, harder and heavier. Some of them join together too. That's why grown-ups have fewer bones than babies – just 206 bones.

Most of your bones will have hardened by the time you are an adult!

My Skull

Your head contains a really big bone called your skull. Your skull is actually made up of lots of little bones joined up together. There is only one bone in your skull that you can move, and that is your jawbone.

The most important job your skull does is to protect your brain. It's your very own safety helmet!

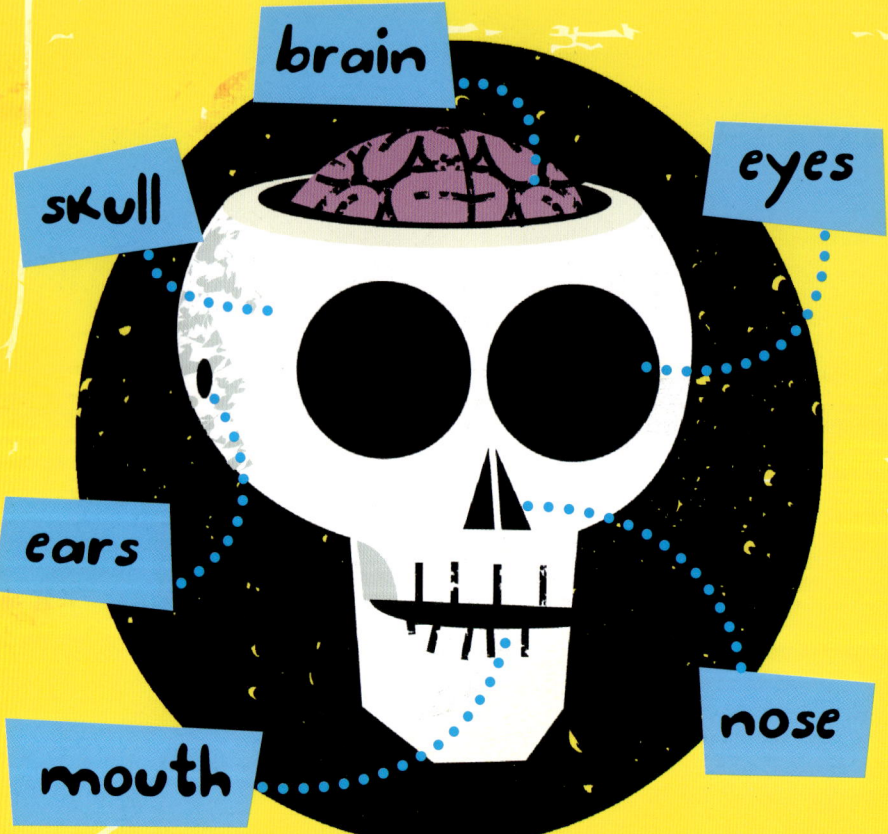

brain

eyes

skull

ears

mouth

nose

Your skull gives your face its shape. Different animals have skulls which are different shapes. This makes their faces different too.

1

Can you guess which skull belongs to which animal?

- mouse
- horse
- lion
- elephant
- rhino

2

3

4

5

1 lion 2 elephant 3 rhino 4 mouse 5 horse

Your skull also contains the tiniest bone inside your body. This bone is inside your ear and is called the stapes (*say* stay-peez). It's about the size of an ant!

My Ribcage

There isn't really a cage inside your chest, but the bones in your chest make it look like that. It's actually a bit like a suit of armour!

Your ribcage protects all the important organs inside it.

The cage is made up of 12 bones on either side called **ribs**.

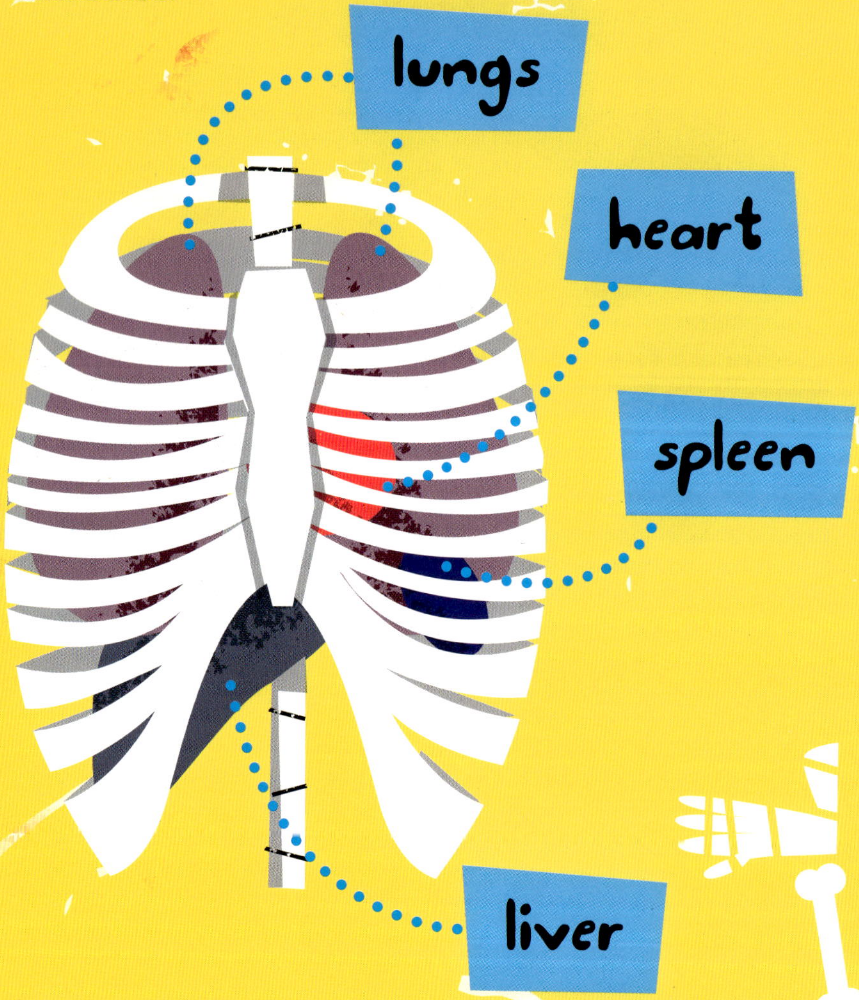

lungs

heart

spleen

liver

At the front the ribs are joined to a bone called the **sternum**.

At the back they are joined to your **spine**, or backbone.

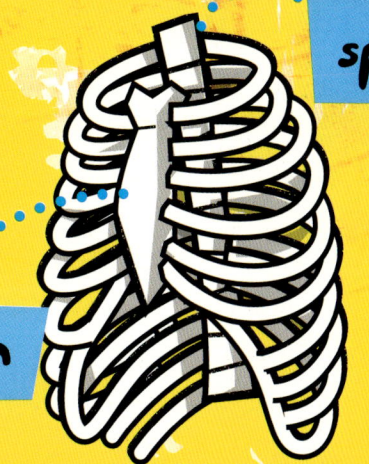

spine

sternum

Skelefact!

The brilliant thing about your ribcage is that it can change shape.

When you breathe in, your ribs lift up and your ribcage gets bigger.

When you breathe out, your ribs move down again and your ribcage gets smaller.

Take a big breath in and out and put your hands on your chest. Can you feel your ribs move?

My Spine

Your spine holds your body up. It's the main reason that you can stand, walk, bend and twist.

Your spine, or backbone, starts at the bottom of your skull. There are 33 bones in your spine, called **vertebrae** (*say* ver-ti-bray). Some of the vertebrae at the bottom of your spine are joined together. The other 24 vertebrae are separate.

These bones are all stacked on top of each other, like a tower of bricks!

Giraffes don't have any more vertebrae in their necks than we do. Their vertebrae are just longer than ours!

giraffe

human

Your spine also protects something called your **spinal cord**. This is a very special bundle of **nerves** that carries messages to and from your brain.

OUCH!

That tickles!

Too hot!

There are many more creatures *without* backbones than *with* them!

13

My Arms and Legs

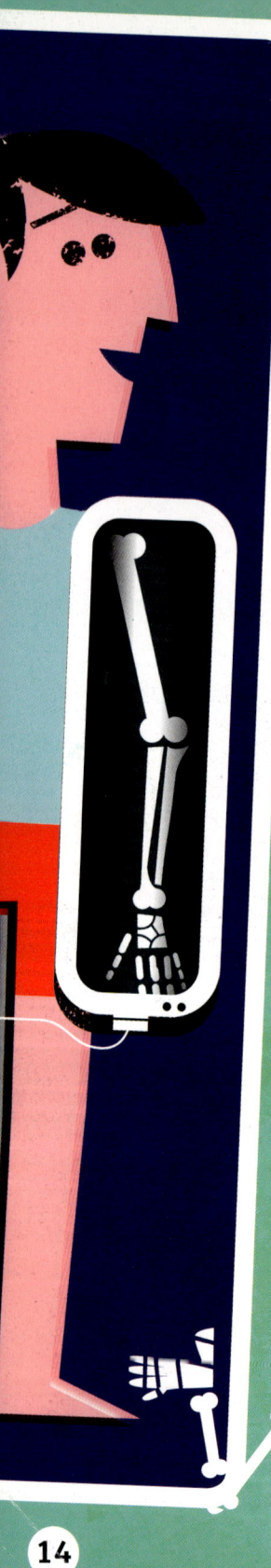

Arms and legs let us move around and do active things!

Your arms are attached to either side of your ribcage. They start at your shoulders and end at your fingers.

radius

humerus

ulna

Most of your arm bones are in your hands because you need to move this part of your body in lots of different ways.

Including your hands, each of your arms contains around 30 different bones! Can you feel all of them?

Your legs are connected to either side of your pelvis. That's the bit you sit on!

They also contain the biggest bone inside your body, called the femur. Your feet have 26 bones each.

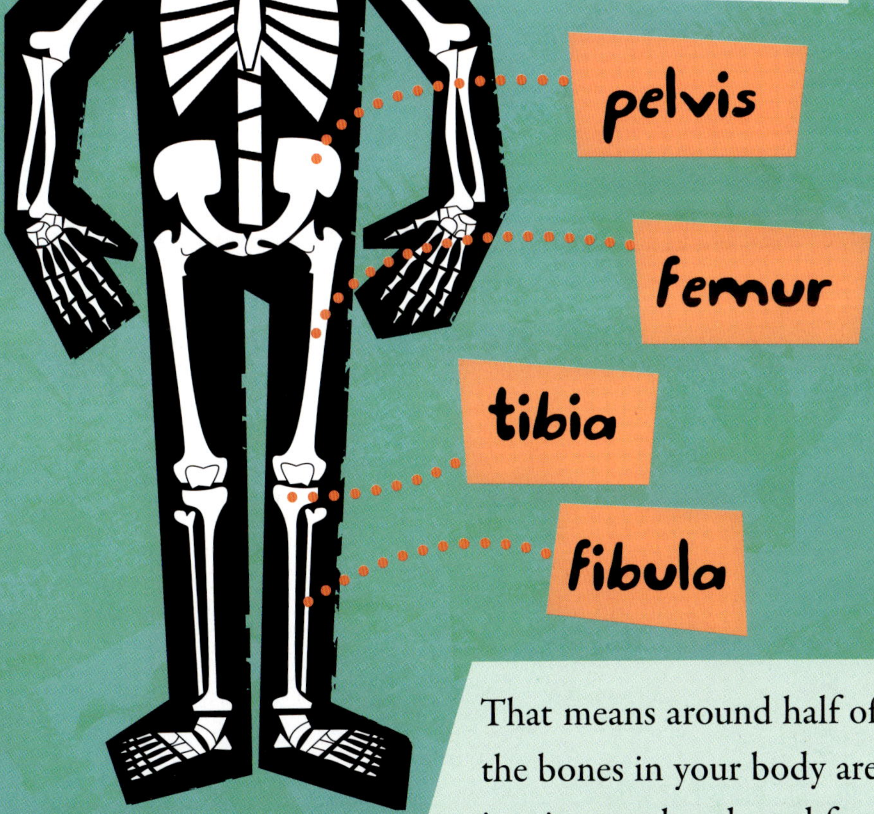

pelvis

femur

tibia

fibula

That means around half of the bones in your body are just in your hands and feet!

My Joints

Joints are the places where two bones connect. Because bones aren't bendy, you need joints so that you can move.

Without them you'd be really stiff!

There are lots of different kinds of joints in your body. Some joints move and some don't.

Joint		Does it move?
elbow		✓
hip		✓
top of neck		✓
small bones of hand		✓
skull		✗

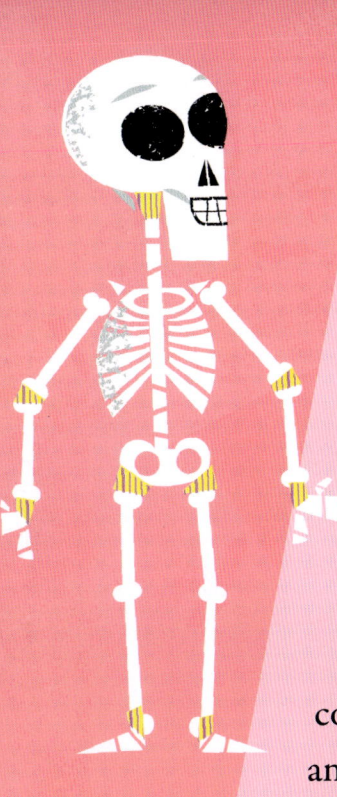

Feel your joints and work out how they move!

The bones in a joint are held together by something called **ligaments**.

Ligaments are like tough rubber bands. They also control the amount that your joints can move. If they didn't do this you could hurt yourself. Have you ever sprained your ankle? That happens when you over-stretch and hurt the ligaments!

Some people are really flexible — that means that their ligaments are more stretchy!

My Muscles

Now we know your skeleton is made of lots of different bones. These bones are joined together at the joints and the joints are held together by ligaments. So what makes it all move?

This is where muscles come in!

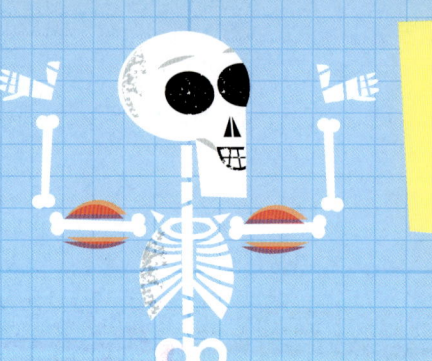

Muscles are made of **protein** and you can find them all over your skeleton.

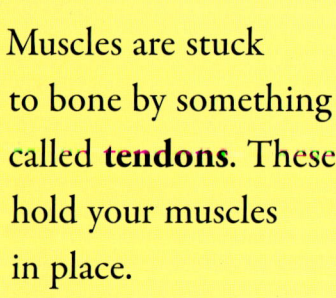

Muscles are stuck to bone by something called **tendons**. These hold your muscles in place.

crab

grasshopper

Did you know some creatures have muscles inside their bones?

What happens when your elbow moves?

1 Your brain wants to make your muscles move. It sends a message to them.

2 The message is carried by your nerves to your muscles.

3 When the muscles around your bones move, your bones move with them.

4 You've bent your elbow!

19

Looking after my Skelebones

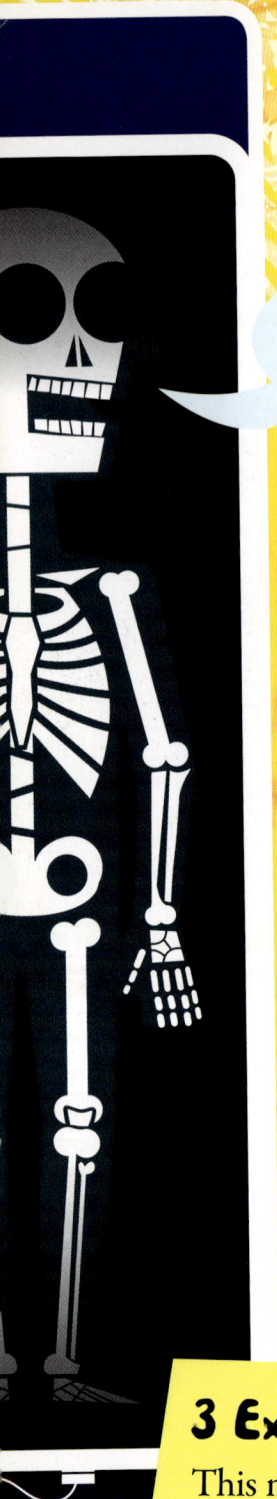

To keep your bones healthy you need ...

1 Calcium

You get this from things like yoghurt, cheese, milk, nuts, cabbage and tofu.

2 Vitamin D

This comes from foods like eggs, fish and cereal. It also comes from sunshine!

3 Exercise

This makes your bones strong and keeps you healthy!

It's great to be active, but you need to be careful not to break any bones! When this happens it's called a fracture. To check it, you may have to have an X-ray. This is a special photograph of your bones. It's just like our special skeleton scanner!

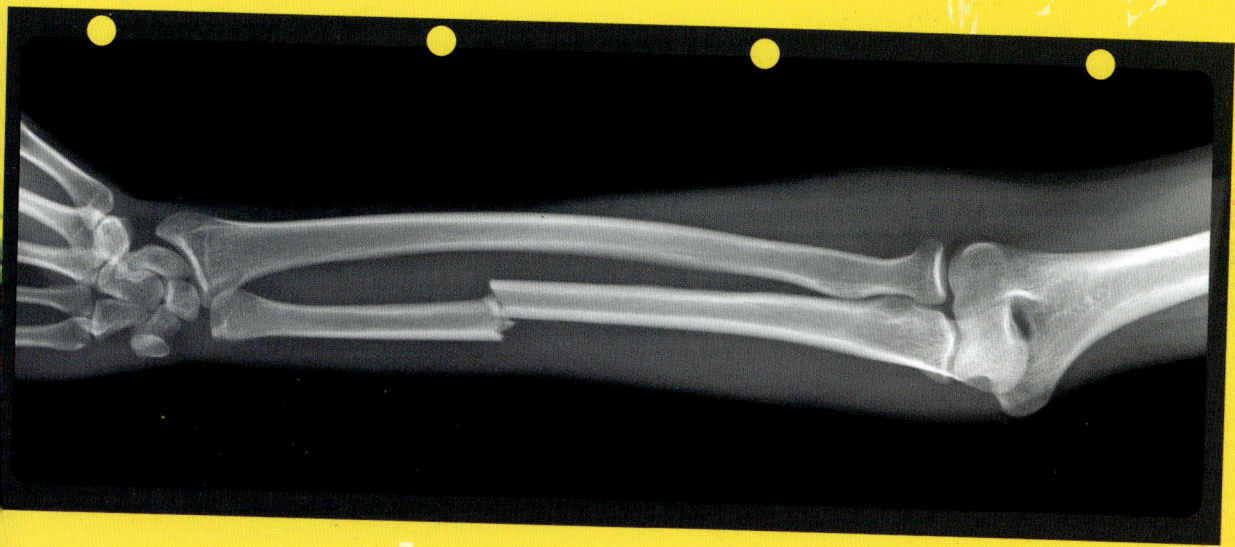

Your brilliant body can fix fractures all by itself. You might need to wear something called a **plaster cast** to hold your bone in place while it heals.

Now you know how to look after your skelebones, go out and have fun!

Glossary

calcium: a mineral found in milk, nuts and tofu that makes your bones hard

cartilage: squashy, bendy bone which can become hard over time

ligaments: strong bands that hold your bones and joints together

muscles: the parts of your body around your bones which make your skeleton move

nerves: connections which carry messages to and from your brain

organs: parts of your body, such as your heart, lungs or liver

plaster cast: a hard case that holds broken bones together so that they can heal

protein: a substance which builds, maintains and replaces the tissues in your body

ribs: bones that form a cage around organs in your chest

spinal cord: a bundle of nerves in your spine connecting your body to your brain

spine: your backbone, which runs from the base of your skull to the bottom of your back

sternum: a flat, T-shaped bone in the middle of your chest

tendons: tough cords which attach your muscles to your bones

vertebrae: a series of small bones that form your spine

vitamin D: a nutrient which helps keep your bones healthy

Index

About the Author

I'm a children's doctor and a TV presenter. I live and work in London, and when I'm not in hospital I travel all over the country making programmes for children and grown-ups.

When I was growing up I wanted to become an astronaut, then a teacher, then I decided to become a doctor. My job is really fun and I like helping people feel better. When I'm not working I like to eat different food, listen to music and dance!

Greg Foot, Series Editor

I've loved science ever since the day I took my papier mâché volcano into school. I filled it with far too much baking powder, vinegar and red food colouring, and WHOOSH! I covered the classroom ceiling in red goo. Now I've got the best job in the world: I present TV shows for the BBC, answer kids' science questions on YouTube, and make huge explosions on stage at festivals!

Working on TreeTops inFact has been great fun. There are so many brilliant books, and guess what ... they're all packed full of awesome facts! What's your favourite?